# 8Voices

## Contemporary Poetry from the American Southwest

by

**Alan Birkelbach, Nathan Brown, Jeffrey DeLotto,
Tony Mares, Ronald E. Moore, Karla K. Morton,
Elizabeth Raby, Gary Swaim**

Edited and Introduction
by
Dan Williams

BASKERVILLE
PUBLISHERS

Baskerville Publishers, Inc.
2455 Halloran Street
Fort Worth, Texas 76107
www.baskervillepublishers.com

Library of Congress Cataloging-in-Publication Data

8 voices : contemporary poetry from the American Southwest / by Alan Birkelbach . . . [et al.] ; edited and Introduction by Dan Williams.
    p. cm.
Includes bibliographical references and index.
ISBN 978-1-880909-79-9 (alk. paper)
    1. Southwest, New—Poetry. 2. American poetry—Southwest, New. 3. American poetry—21st century. 4. American poetry—20th century. I. Birkelbach, Alan. II. Williams, Dan. III. Title: Eight voices : contemporary poetry from the American Southwest. IV. Title: Contemporary poetry from the American Southwest.
    PS566.A13 2012
    811'.6080979—dc23
                                    2012038378

Manufactured in the United States of America

First Printing, 2012

# Introduction

*8 Voices* is as an act of liberation. The eight voices included in this volume share a sense of frustration at being categorized as regional poets. And not just any region. Living and writing in Texas and the Southwest, they are generally typecast as western poets, a label that is sometimes misperceived into suggesting verse packed with the conventions of cowboy poetry. Frustrated by the expectations of readers unacquainted with Texas and the Southwest, they collaboratively envisioned a volume that would demonstrate the remarkable span and scope of their poetry to readers accustomed to hackneyed images and mawkish sentimentality. They wanted to demonstrate that there was more to western poetry than wild horses, branding irons, arrowheads, and creaking windmills.

Their frustration is understandable. Regionalism necessarily implies boundaries and confinement. As a number of cultural critics have recently argued, regionalism is a discourse that inevitably involves power relations between a center and outlying areas, and what is situated on the margins is often perceived to be marginal. When the rural is contrasted with the urban, the country with the city, there is often a suggestion of a hierarchy of values and value judgments, as the word urbanity implies. This has been especially true in American culture when eastern and western were used as labels to indicate contrasting degrees of refinement and civility. Distance from eastern cultural centers often led to specious presumptions of lesser elegance and sophistication. At times, such distance insinuated "a setting outside of modern development, a zone of backwardness where locally variant folkways still prevail" (Brodhead 115). When pronounced by the eastern cultural elite, classification as a regional writer was a dismissive and condescending critique.

Such critical pronouncements, of course, are ludicrous. For well over a century American writers have demonstrated not only that all great writing is thoroughly grounded in a sense of place but also that regionalism subverts the skewed judgments of distant critics by establishing an alternate set of critical criteria. In making use of specific locality, in evoking the various landscapes, characters, dialects, and customs that distinguish a place, all great writing confirms that value judgments are contextual and that the local can serve as an imaginative springboard to the universal.

All of the eight poets in this volume are regional poets who proudly acknowledge, and celebrate, their sense of place. They desire to be liberated—not from the landscapes they inhabit—but from the labels and presuppositions that categorize and limit them. They each have a strong sense of place, yet they each, in different ways, explore territories, vistas, and realms far beyond the geography that surrounds them. This is true even when writing about a dry creek bed or a desert mountain peak in Texas or the Southwest. Whether writing about the near or the distant, the physical or the metaphysical, these eight poets share a unique talent to transport readers into the strange, striking landscapes of the faraway, places where readers are overcome by sudden and powerful perceptions.

Poetry is an imaginative journey. I think of each poem included in this volume as an exploration, and the range and depth of what is explored is truly remarkable. Readers can journey to distant points around the globe, and indeed circle the globe. They can venture from the contemporary all the way back into the prehistory when the earth was fierce, volcanic, and alien. In reading the poems contained in these pages, they can explore the nature of language, the nature of art, and the nature of love; they can, in fact, explore human nature. Collectively, the eight voices examine an extensive range of human emotions, from the loss of a daughter to an awakening into the unfamiliar after six months in a coma. There is fear, loss, and disillusionment, but there is also courage, passion, and faith. There is isolation and longing, but there is also intimacy and serenity. More than anything else, *8 Voices* demonstrates not only the power of the imagination to transport, but also to atone.

The poets who make up *8 Voices* are each quite unique, having richly diverse backgrounds, professions, and interests. Their distinct personalities are evident in their distinct voices and styles, which draw from a surprisingly wide range of experiences, observations, and perceptions. But there is one thing they all share—a highly developed level of craft and poetics. In their own unique ways, each poet displays an exemplary degree of linguistic control and poetic skill. Their poems are richly metaphoric, allusive, and rhythmical. For the most part, they do not adhere to conventional meters and rhyme schemes, yet they are tightly structured and arranged, revealing a deep familiarity with the technical practices, forms, and traditions of poetry. Reading their poems, particularly reading them aloud, reveals that they share a highly developed sensitivity to both the sound and sense of language. Their lines are graceful, nuanced, and lyrical, and yet they are also accessible and readable.

When required to read poetry in their literature surveys, college students often express frustration and irritation. Recently I asked some students why, in general, they had such negative attitudes about poetry. A few responded that their high school experiences were less than pleasant, but one young woman offered what I thought was a particularly interesting remark. She stated that her distaste for poetry was because most poems, especially contemporary poems, seemed too private, esoteric, and cryptic to understand: "It's like there's a party going on, and I'm not invited." Many people today seem to share this attitude. There is a general sense that, to be good, poems must be abstract and enigmatic, that poets are indeed enjoying private affairs with only a few invited guests. The poetry of *8 Voices*, however, invites everyone to the party. One of its greatest strengths is that, as they are interesting, engaging, and pleasing to read, the poems are approachable and comprehensible. Here there are no private affairs. Each of the eight poets offers poems that appeal to readers to pause, reflect, and enjoy.

Such inviting openness is, I believe, crucial in poetry today. For the most part, poetry no longer has a broad popular appeal. In his often reprinted essay, "Can Poetry Matter," Dana Gioia declares: "American poetry now belongs to a subculture. No longer part of the mainstream of artistic and intellectual life, it has become the specialized occupation of a relatively small and isolated group" (219). Although ironically it thrives as a subculture, poetry does not matter to most people—and yet it should. Each of the eight poets included in *8 Voices* wants a broad range of readers to appreciate what they read. They want their poetry to matter—not just to other poets—but to all readers. In a world saturated with the temptations and distractions of the internet, in a world where reading anything other than text messages seems arduous, *8 Voices* offers poetry that is not only readable, but relevant.

In a remark to Thomas Wentworth Higginson, Emily Dickinson defined what for her was the essence of poetry: "If I read a book and it makes my whole body so cold no fire can ever warm me, I know that is poetry. If I feel physically as if the top of my head were taken off, I know that is poetry. These are the only ways I know it. Is there any other way?" When I read the poetry submitted for the *8 Voices* project for the first time, I experienced some of those poignant, powerful moments Dickinson described as poetry. Sometimes after reading a poem I would feel so deeply affected that I would simply stop and stare at the page, frozen, feeling numb to everything around me except the words in front of me. I felt deeply moved, jolted as if the top of my head had been wrenched off. At times I was so powerfully moved that I was in two places at one time, both in my comfortable reading chair and in a strange, striking place landscape where the poet had transported me. Psychologists and educators refer to these moments of insight and discovery as cognitive shifts, when two distinct thoughts or feelings combine to create a sudden and new awareness. I think that the strength of *8 Voices,* its essential relevance, is its ability to urge readers into these moments of insight and discovery. The poetry of *8 Voices* does not offer solutions to war, poverty, and misery. Yet each of the eight poets offer poems that can spark the imagination and provoke reflection. In his poem, "Of Asphodel, That Greeny Flower," WC Williams declares:

It is difficult
To get the news from poems
Yet men die miserably every day
For lack
Of what is found there.

What is found in poetry is quite often what is lost elsewhere, glimpses of the fantastic, the bizarre, the exultant, the passionate, the marvelous, and the magical. Here in *8 Voices* there are numerous poems that sustain and nurture us with such glimpses, allowing us to feel what is deeply human but rarely expressed. These glimpses are not an antidote to the troubles and terrors that darken our horizons, yet they are a crucial indemnity that counterbalances all that we dread. They are a means of preserving our souls. Taking time to read poetry is not a waste of time; it is a way of escaping the daily demands of time by allowing us to experience imaginatively what is meaningful, heartfelt, and essential within us. Good poetry ignites our creative thought and allows us to feel, perceive, and empathize in ways we could not otherwise. We are in desperate need of good poetry.

That *8 Voices* is good poetry I have no doubt. I have gained much by becoming acquainted with the poems included in this volume, and I feel privileged to have read them. I believe that anyone who picks up this volume will feel the same.

References

Brodhead, Richard H. *Culture of Letters: Scenes of Reading and Writing in Nineteenth-Century America*. Chicago: University of Chicago Press, 1993.

Fetterly, Judith, and Marjorie Pryse. *Writing Out of Place: Regionalism, Women, and American Literary Culture*. Urbana: University of Illinois Press, 2003.

Gioia, Dana. "Can Poetry Matter?" http://www.danagioia.net/essays/ecpm.htm

Joseph, Phillip. *American Regionalism in a Global Age*. Baton Rouge: Louisiana State University Press, 2007

Dan Williams is Director of TCU Press and a Professor in the TCU English Department. A specialist in early national print culture, he has published four books and over fifty articles and essays in his scholarly field. He is also the managing editor for *descant*, the Fort Worth literary journal, and publishes a broadside series. Although a closet poet, he recently had a novel accepted for publication.

# Table of Contents

## Jeffrey DeLotto

## Tony Mares

## Ronald E. Moore

## Karla K. Morton

## Elizabeth Raby

## Gary Swaim

# Alan Birkelbach

The 2005 Texas Poet Laureate, is the author of nine books of poetry. He is a winner of the 2010 North Texas Book Festival Award, two-time presenter at the Texas Book Festival, a Spur, Wrangler, Pushcart, and TIL Children's Book award nominee, and a finalist in the 2012 Next Generation Indie Book Awards. He is a native Texan.

# Prime Heart

It is the terrible perfection
of its symmetry that gives us pause.
It seems there is no end
to it, a cathedral that

is never done.  How fleshy might it
yet get, its meat still quivering from
providential cause?  What
triggered this heart to beat,

the moist chambers to pulse?  To create
such a dichotomous thing from such
a base origin, to
culture from the darkest

reviled root this bilateral beast
requires a wise and careful mover.
It governs structure deep,
and deeper still, beyond

histology, past disposition,
when we are finally torn, and torn again
in half, our heart laid bare,
exposed, all too aware

of that galvanic machinery
that powers all, our meager spark,
our pure connectedness, our
dreadful anatomy.

# En Route

There, past the bridge,
at the edge of the row of houses,
just emerging from the tangle of trees,

the bobcat waited.
I stopped the car, stared at him
for several seconds, hesitated,

then reached down for my camera.
By the time I looked back up
that space was empty.

He had already
crossed the road
and was a hundred yards away.

There were lots of
unspoken commands
filling that stretch of moments.

Later, maybe today,
maybe next week,
sometime soon,

I will take a walk past the bridge,
at the edge of the row of houses,
and find myself just emerging from the tangle of trees.

When I am standing there,
tufted ears twitching,
don't wait to take my picture.

If you look away for even a second
I will only be a golden blur
far along the path.

# Death Goes Courting

Damn how he kept getting reimagined.
Things were much easier in the Charon days:
there was always money in the bank,
People came to him, all he had to do was row, row, row.
And then there was the heyday of the Black Death.
Well, sure, he'd been mis-portrayed on the tarot cards,
there was that, (and Lord knows every cliché of a gypsy
and bad horror writer had come to depend on that interpretation),
and it still made him feel queasy remembering the day
when the x-ray was invented. It was like looking at himself
in the mirror Every. Single. Day. But Death was Death. And
He was Death. And everything wore out and got ground down
or burned up or torn up or made into something else.
There was no moral compass to it, regardless of how
he was illustrated. He had checked once and nope, there was
no umbilicus that attached a soul to a skeleton. He had looked all over,
checked each patella and phalange.
God and Soul and Death—all separate things.
Man never did get it, never could reconcile it,
always wanted to put some extra meaning on it,
flesh it all up with emotion, make it softer, ease everyone into it.
So, here he was, trying to look as dignified as possible,
(were his ribs straight?), flowers in one hand,
teeth showing as friendly as possible,
about to let this woman know,
in his socially inconvenient way,
how seriously he planned on dating her,
how he was intent on making her his own.

# Finding the Old Soda Pop Bottle

Thinking about whose lips
have curled around the rim
of this bottle solves nothing.

It won't rebury important remains,
or distribute medicine,
or make anyone wave a flag like a revolutionary.

But I can think how this bottle was
small and perfect for a woman's hand,
how a man bought it for her without her asking.

How a single bead of sweat might have
glistened like a pearl
down her swan-like neck,

How her print dress, blown by a hot wind, hugged her thighs.
How she closed her eyes in satisfaction.
How she licked her lips.

# Quiet Calamity

She looked at me as if I was insane
when I bought the small package
of three small chalkboards taped together
but would not cut it open.

Something might be sleeping there
and even if it isn't we can still have some respect
Aren't excavation sites always quiet I asked?
What syllables might be a secret in this bundle?

She should understand this.
I have told her a million times
that I like to watch her bring her hair up
in that kind of nonchalant-twirly way all women have

Without looking, staring into nothing,
she sticks a hairpin in it,
and, like a hummingbird,
the hair shouldn't stay up there but it does.

And later, that night,
when we are watching t.v. on the sofa
and are on our third glass of wine
and her legs are draped across my legs

she will reach up to remove that pin.
She will shake her head.
Stars will shiver in the heavens.
And whole cities will fall.

# Jesus's Dog

You have to let me go. I'm done. Worn out.
I've done the things a dog should do—or want
to do. Not even you can keep me young.
Can you see me? You have kept my heart
and legs strong. I have no pain, no torn
ears or worried pads. Over the years
you've fixed my hips and dropped the cataracts
right off my eyes like scales. No flea nor tick
dares bite me. No food disagrees. Your hands
make sure my breath is eucalyptus fresh,
my teeth are clean, my coat still shines like silk.
I've seen whole tribes of cats come and go
I've fathered more generations of dull puppies than I can remember.
I quit worrying about whether
things were clean or unclean. And so did you.
But People are already talking. And whatever's out
there now is bigger than my growl—and don't
think that's not hard to say. I'm tired. There's nothing
else that I can bark about. Yes,
I confess, I would beg for you
to stroke me. Dogs beg, that what we do. But it's
not like begging for alms. I would beg
for a bone, a scrap of bread, for you
to scratch behind my ear just so and yes,
sometimes, just for you to rub your hands
along the crown of my head, down my quivering
back. I liked that charge, that humming, healing
song in your hands that thrummed too low
for even me to hear. I never felt
that I deserved those gifts—but I would
always ask for them. And you were there.
I was a dog. I was your dog.
But there is a season for everything. You know that.

And no, you cannot make it so I
will live forever. You cannot leave me to
your mother. You know why. (She sees more angels
than there are magicians in Egypt.)
We've been here before, at this moment,
sometimes by sheer stupidity,  sometimes
by circumstance (you know all about
that—or will anyway), and sometimes
just by the grinding stone of days and years.
Today it is different.  Now, one last hug
and hold my head.  Here, I will lick your hand.
I love you Master for that is what you are
but I am longing to lie down, right over there,
and sleep in that final sunny spot.

# Fiesta Skirt

Her skirt made every man a bad dancer.
It was a colored windmill that hypnotized us
and she knew it.

She casually walked up and down the row of us,
holding our arms for her balance
to show how her boots had been polished.

She did a few practice whirls,
burning spirals in our eyes,
spinning galaxies sweeter than night skies.

We knew this was an old smile and bow.
We still regretted every dance class
we'd skipped to go swimming.

Of course, we knew if we got close enough to her dark curls
we'd smell a perfume on her
that would have us undone.

Like whiskery, rooted sunflowers
our bodies tilted toward her all evening,
faces open, bobbing, and hopeful.

Our minds were full of graceful phrases we'd never utter.
Our tongues were as useless as bones in drought.
Our toes lost the ability to tap.

# Living South of Sonora

It's a given the forms
your mind can attach a sound to.
We're taught each thing
has its own syllabus of noise

Possums, raccoons, skunks—
they're huggers and pushers,
using their body and shoulders;
sniffing, washing—innocent diggers.

Most birds are just visiting
in a pecking kind of way.
Horned lizards bare-palm stones.
Prairie dogs dig with alert abandon.

All manners of creature:
even some man in the dark
that's lost and just shambling through—
your ear can prick and dismiss it.

But there are other noises you can't place:
maybe a screech or a loud scratch,
a branch that screams in bending—but doesn't break,
something that splashes where there isn't water.

Some noises you don't explore after.
You leave the night door shut.
The flashlight might reveal an odd glistening,
some shambling bulk that isn't afraid.

You decide you aren't ready to find
those things bold enough to give themselves away,
faces assimilated into the stones,
roots that don't mind being submerged.

There may be pools out there your feet aren't aware of,
currents full of strange phonics,
tassled with creatures floating at the right hand of mermaids,
waiting patiently for you to get lured in.

# Raising Dust on Caddo Peak

"When it doesn't rain, we water,
pumping the purest water three hundred feet
straight up from nothing we've ever seen..."
from 'Making Book on the Aquifer' Walt McDonald

In this drought geologists say we can't drill deep enough.
There's cactus then rock,
then shale, then rock,
then nothing.

It's hard to imagine
one day fish swam here,
but I can stir up fossils with my boot;
it's mute evidence enough.

Witching's a wasted art;
might as well let the hazel gather dust.
Cows wander off their paths,
their noses not leading them in any direction.

Snakes don't bother pushing venom,
Baby's feet are safe from scorpions that don't strike.
Raccoons give up washing.
Acorns break down, dry as chaff.

There's no squint sharp enough
to see clouds past the horizon,
not even up here on this forgotten tower,
not even this close to God's unweeping eye.

# The Red Panther Petroglyph at Lake Amistad

We might as well be cutting sod
with a straight spade for all this wonder.
But there's no bog men here to marvel on,
no bronzed or musky bones, or bowls of skulls
that once held fires similar to our own,
no table of tannic threads, no interrupted slumber.

As if this stone would take a spade.
It's harder than the years we think we've
counted. There's no resisting or moving
it. Its asterism is locked in. It
accepts our boots like it has accepted
everything else. But even with the immobility

this painting never rests. To have
our hearts be still we have to look then
leave. This cat leaps and leaps again each time
we blink, a curving, red, and fierce design
we can translate with terror well enough,
a taloned, dread discovery that snags us in our sleep.

# Thunderstorm Outside of Lamesa

On that treeless plain
the storms can come out of nowhere,
big, black things that
chew up the horizon in minutes.

You don't stand outside
to thank God for rain.
The raindrops are full of grit.
the lightning is fickle.

But the ghost that stands watch
in the small old cemetery
at the edge of the yard
never leaves her spot.

She ignores the hailstones
that fall through her.
She doesn't wipe her forehead
or pull back sopping hair.

She looks at me and points west
always trying to remind me
the hot, dry wind will be back,
reclaiming what it owns.

# Walking the Dry Swimming Hole

We walk this dry riverbed as if we had sense.
We've seen rain water rise up faster
than calves could scramble.
watched them bawl and be swept away,
their mothers knee—then chest—deep,
as helpless as we were just watching.

We've seen seasons so wet
the water flowed from the riverbank,
cool from the folds of the earth,
streams called by Aaron's rod,
flavored by mint, wild berries,
sweet enough to bless our face in.

Today we stop at the bottom of the swimming hole
we've splashed a thousand times,
replaying the summer days
when we touched bottom on a dare,
bringing up rocks from the bottom
just to prove we could.

We were certain then
the water would flow forever,
knowing we would always dive here,
like pale angels into the mossy green,
our arms holding us in place,
our cheeks puffy with wide-eyed, holy breath.

# Home Movie

"And these brittle prints, our own grandparents and parents like a time warp."
From 'Turn Around, Turn Around' Walt McDonald

The old film chatters through the projector
like crows who have seen the future.
Some nights when it's still
a hundred degrees outside
I play the movie again and again.
My father smiled more then.
I was finding my first steps,
my arms reaching for gravity's handles.

A thousand times growing up
I have seen my father plow
the fields that surround this house.
Now it's all fallen on me—
so I get up every morning
to make the tractor cough
and walk through his images
that fill the rows.

But during nights like this
the heat makes everything stop.
The owls give up diving for mice.
The snakes think their tongues
are cooler in their mouths.
Death sits on a bale in the barn,
wipes his forehead with old gingham,
decides some things can wait.

He hears the sputter of the projector,
smiles when he imagines the last laughter,
the people there pointing at the camera,
and then the bright white ending.
And he knows, every night, like a prayer,
I will turn the projector toward a window
and for a long time, before everything sleeps,
I will let that light shine out into the darkness
as far as it will reach.

# The Contract

This is something you did last night
while I was smoking my pipe
on the patio and writing.
As I remember it was a
Danish pipe and a Cavendish blend
and the words were coming as they always did,
like old companions who knew their way up the stairs,
who had a key, who didn't mind the smoke.
I imagine you were curled up on your sofa,
after a day full of nibbling tasks.
Or maybe you were already in bed,
your legs making little tents.
Either way you chose the company of my book
instead of the ten o'clock news.
You wanted something that would put you to sleep.
but, unbeknownst to you,
I only wanted to wave a document in your face
and ask a lot of questions.
But it's okay. These are questions you can sleep with,
like someone who's lonely
asking whether someone loves them,
if they will be there in the morning.
Read a few pages, imagine me, then set the book down.
This is the way we should go to sleep.
We are old friends now.
You have already visualized the way
the body shifts as it goes up the steps,
the way the key reacts in a lock,
the way the clouds hang heavy over the syllables.
We should always end the day together
with this type of measured breathing,
with the wisps of our imagining
eventually drifting off into the world.

# Nathan Brown

is a musician, photographer and award-winning poet from Norman, Oklahoma. He holds a PhD from the University of Oklahoma, but mostly travels now, performing readings and concerts, as well as leading workshops and speaking on creativity and the need for readers to not give up on poetry. He's published eight books. *Karma Crisis: New and Selected Poems* came out this spring. And a previous book, *Two Tables Over*, won the *2009 Oklahoma Book Award*.

# The Sign

She comes in—tanned, tight jeans,
bleach-blond hair down the back,
blue eyes and too much makeup—

with a baby on her hip. And I'd
decided already what this poem
was going to be about, when she

sits down across from what looks
to be her father and begins to sign
with her one free hand. He smiles

and signs back—hands rolling effusively,
lips moving in a soundless poetry.
Their gazes trade loves back and forth.

The baby's eyes glow in the wave
and trickle of mom's fingers that must
look like birds close enough to touch.

And the trusses of my preconceptions
begin to buckle. The edges of prejudice
begin to crumble like dry toast...

and...        I have made a mistake.

I want to go over and apologize,
but I don't know the sign for that.

# Go the Spoils

We measure cohabitation
by the consolidation
of previous divisions
of stuff.

When her pillows come in,
my old ones will go.

Her TV, sleek, wide
and filled with plasma
will surely replace mine,
    all 100 pounds of it
    with buzzing tubes
    and a burnt transistor.

In the divorce ten years ago,
the one who left me, left me
with the house and its payments
but took the bed, most of the dishes,
the kitchen table and a bottle of Clorox.

I got the classic literature and poetry.
I don't remember a fight over that.

She kept the daughter of course.

But today, unloading this one's boxes,
I noticed we both owned copies
of the movie *Dumb and Dumber*.

I suggested we toss one.

*But who will get it then*, she asked,
*when we split up?*

*You, babe. I promise.*
*It's yours.*

# What Good Am I?

We sit down to our daily specials
and an orange tar pit of goo they claim
is queso here at Big Truck Tacos,

and her 14-year-old lips part to the question
So Dad, are weed and marijuana the same thing?

And my narrowing esophagus confirms
that it is in fact goo, and not queso,
as I sputter, then cough a time or two.

When I pull the napkin from my lips,
I swear it was the goo that caused this
and not her perfectly reasonable inquiry.

She smiles, pats me on the back, and says,
It's okay, Dad. It was just a question.

> I've grown accustomed to her calm adultness.
> Something life required of her early on,
> for reasons I'd rather not get into.

And as I try to recompose myself, scraping
a dollop of "queso" off my sleeve,
I tell her, *I think so, Honey.*

> I hold a PhD and honestly don't know.
> I've never known my crack from my crank,
>     the spoon from the needle,
>         or what goes in the pipe.

> And I realize this ignorance, for some,
> calls into question my status as "poet."

> But this is the first time
> it's rendered me useless
> as a father.

# Mixed Messages

The young yoga instructor
comes into the Red Cup
as often as the poets
who write in its corners.

Her smile verges on absence.
Her posture, immaculate.
And her lack of any makeup
has a fierce deliberateness to it.

Yet, the concern she often carries
for making a statement with this
has pulled her forehead up some
and drawn the sockets of her eyes
down to the point that she might
need to reconsider the mission.

Today she sits spread-eagled,
feet bouncing on the rungs
of the barstools to each side,
her body inviting something in
that her face seems to push away.

But she is reading with blue eyes
a small yellow book on Hinduism.
Her smoothie is a bright green.
And her long auburn hair,
uncombed with a vengeance,
is gathered into a stout ponytail
that swishes to Coldplay's latest hit

like some wand waving
through the dark cloud
of her confusion
and honesty.

# The Sangre de Cristos

The bloodshot eyes
of Christ's dark mountains
look down on the City of Holy Faith.

Their ears have grown weary
but still wait for any melody,
even the slightest strains
of some hopeful song
for a wayfaring heart.

But the gentle voice
that slides between the lips
of these lonesome valleys
whispers through the trees
and low-hanging clouds
prayers upon prayers
that pulse with deep love
and a patient sadness,

calling on all who suffer
at their dry, cracked feet
to heal the bruised
and bleeding sides
of these sacred hills.

# 2201 Dakota St.

Such a humble brick box now,
here on the small street behind
our old house on Morgan Drive.

I don't think I've ever seen it
from the front like this. Strange.

All I remember are two sisters,
    especially the older one,
bouncing on an old trampoline
in the backyard catty-cornered to ours,
bouncing and laughing in cut-offs
and bright pink bikini tops.

I could see them floating up
above the pointed wood fence
when I'd hang out in our yard
pretending to work on a bike
or the mower.
                I could see them
and the trampoline too, though,
from the window of my upstairs room.

Sometimes they'd stop the bouncing
and just lie there like toast in the sun.

And there are no dreams more earnest
than the daydreams of a teenaged
Baptist preacher's son, who's still,
at this point, trying to be a good
Baptist preacher's son.

Such a cruel hormonal torture
in the shadows and dark rooms
of the twentieth century.

And I never thought back then to think
that Satan and Job might be out there,
somewhere, chortling their asses off.

God... I imagine... however...
might have been more reserved.

# That Black & White of Bukowski

A black skillet squats
on a white stove top,
the Schilling black pepper
and Morton salt up there
above his left shoulder
on the old Frigidaire.

The thumb and middle finger
of his right hand pinch a cigarette
sucked down to a limp thread
of ashes dangling from its butt
while the index finger between them
points somewhere to the right of my face.

The poems must have been selling by this point.

He's got a wristwatch and an imported beer,
both down at the end of his left arm.
His belly's beginning to push
at the buckle of his belt.

And the acne vulgaris
has retreated, mostly,
behind a graying beard
and large folds of skin
that curve up and around
a big smile and squinted eyes.

The big smile, of course,
being the best evidence
that he was over the hump
and headed for the finish line.

# My Juniors and Seniors

It's the usual university mix.
Quite a few more girls than guys.
Around half are smiling. A few
staring at the floor.

But all of them looking like
they've had a massive rug
pulled out from under them
that they never knew was there.

They sense, but can't yet declare,
that a well-dressed someone,
with incomprehensible assets
and balances in foreign banks,

just donned a hat and waltzed off
into the morning fog of Zurich
with their futures securely locked
in his patent leather briefcase,

in search of the highest bidder.

# Somalia's Children

I hear reports of you
and sometimes see it
on ABC World News
accompanied by statistics
and the science of starvation.

Your legs the size of my forearms.
Your eyes like yellow eggs
melting into a dying sun.

And yours is a portrait
I cannot paint. There is
no spectrum of colors
to mix into the tints
and hues of your anguish.

So,
this poem is merely to honor
the absence of the words
that would not honor
the memory
of your gruesome beauty.

# Venom

She was a woman of surpassing beauty.

... Cassius speaking of Cleopatra, c. 210 to 230 CE

No rest for the beautiful.

But especially
for those of surpassing
wealth and beauty.

Wrestling Caesars
for power. Everyone
in and out of their togas
all the time. A son here,
a few others over there.

Her bath in fresh goat's milk.

His battle at sea.
His suicide after the loss.

Then, the snap of fangs,
the bites
        of two asps,
as tradition demands,

and they all fall down.

# Unlike Father, Unlike Son

> My God, my God, why hast thou forsaken me?
>
> ... Jesus of Nazareth

There were days
he didn't want the job.

Remember the cup
in the garden, that stuff
he did not want to drink?

But his dad made him
down it anyway?

It's tough to live
with a father like that.

You're about to save the world
and everywhere you go,
all the restaurants, theaters
and bars, everyone always
just wants to talk to him.

Maybe that's why Mary
cried at the foot of the cross.

She knew how long it would take
for people to realize her son
was a better man
than his father.

# As a Dying Man Always Does

... Lorenzo the Magnificent, 1492

Ask for one last margarita,
with salt,

    and for the window
    to be opened wide.

Tell the king to go to hell,

    and to your sister say
    you never much cared for
    her husband or that middle son.

Have someone light a candle,

    maybe fluff the pillows
    one more time.

Demand a shot of tequila, straight,
to wash down the margarita

    as you rip the needles
    and tubes out of your veins.

Go silent...
for a time...

    and hope that your daughter
    doesn't want you to go, yet.

Then,
for God's sake,

    think of one
    last thing
    to say.

# Shift

Nevertheless it moves.

... Galileo, 1642

You took away our center,
my good man, moved us
out and away from
the command post
of God's universe.

You stuck a bright star,
a burning ball
with no soul,
in its place.

How did you think
the cardinals and bishops would react,

after they'd gone to all that trouble
having those elaborate gowns tailored,
not to mention the expense
of those gaudy hats?

Maybe at 69 you began to see
a certain allure in the conditions
of house arrest.

I'm only 46 and I'll tell you,
it's crossed my mind a time or two.

Maybe you saw more
in that telescope
than you could tell us.

Either way, the more I mull
your defiant last words,

the more I want to say them
out loud to everyone I meet.

## Existential Solstice

This—the day that offers
the least amount of light—
rates as my favorite of the year...
this day and the hundred or so
that fall right before.

Nothing too philosophical about it,
except maybe that I smell more beauty
in the winter of things.

Spring tosses out dangerous promises
like rose petals at a white wedding.

But autumn's slow leak into December
teaches us to hold hands
as we come to grips with endings...

with where the inevitable swings
of the planet's axis are taking us.

## Between Two Artists

Dear God,
         I have always admired
your work. And were it not for that,
I wouldn't bother you with this. But,

I must say that your installation piece
at the Point Lobos Nature Reserve
above Big Sur simply goes too far.

The Monterey pines are too tall,
the cypresses too fanned out in perfection
from trunks tied in intricate knots
that would take centuries
to unravel.
                The cliffs appear
superimposed for dramatic effect
with impossible jags giving way
to fairytale caves that burst forth gushes
of blue water like a French soda topped
with a spray of whipped cream.

The crash of waves and explosions of foam
are too much like a Disneyland ride.
There are too many kinds of birds, too many
varieties of plants, and too much color
in both, I might add.

In short, it lacks integrity.
It does not speak to the truth
of the way things are. And I don't think
that viewers will trust, or believe,
its authenticity.

# Jeffrey DeLotto

Professor of English at Texas Wesleyan University, teaches writing and British literature. He has also taught writing and literature at Texas Tech University, at Yarmouk University (in Jordan), and as a Fulbright Lecturer in Bulgaria. His books include *Voices at the Door Days of a Chameleon: Collected Poems*, and *Voices Writ in Sand: Dramatic Monologues and Other Poems*. His poems, essays and stories have appeared in numerous magazines, journals and anthologies.

# Rousse

Trimontium Hotel Bar
Plovdiv, Bulgaria, 1992


Nosdrave. It is like "prozt" or "cheers,"
But we are Bulgarians and see cheer in
Nothing—so, nosdrave, yes, you say it
Very well (perhaps from that CIA training,
Eh?) Give it a bit of a slur, as after your
Seventh glass of rakia, our brandy, and
With a look, too, at a man to say "ask me
No questions," at a woman to mean "we
Could make tragic and ecstatic love when
Your husband goes to work." You have
Been around—I have always an eye for
Such things—but to understand the soul
Of a prostitute, to understand the honest
Smile of pleasure in the mirror, believe it
So he will, too—<u>that</u> is to understand the
Bulgarian soul, but understand that we
Will later know and hate ourselves for
Believing the smile but smile again the
Next day....How can you understand us?
America: on top, bowing to no one, bending
Over for no one's soldiers, can know little
Of us, always in the middle in the way to
Somewhere, between the power, the Turks,
The Germans ho, ho, the Bulgarian luck,
(We chose them in both wars), the Russians,
Now you—and we clap you on the back as
Our benefactors at last, just as we did the
Soviets a few years before. Here, let me
Tell you: I heard you went to the village of
Khrojna to kill a pig, a real Bulgarian
Folk Christmas, eh? How did I...? Rousse
Hears things—never mind. You went with
Christova, a professor from the university, and
Tchalakov, a very merry fellow, talks English

Without a fault, well, he should—he was boss
Of the English Language Institute ten years
Ago, for our masters, and would report any
One of his students to the police if he heard
The student had even spoken to an American
Or a Brit for any reason, for "sympathizing"—
You know what happened to them? That was
Not Tchalakov's business—he was a favorite.
You would not guess it from how happy he
Seemed with your company....Most of us were
No different; we are no different now. So,
Another glass—nosdrave, my friend.

# Al-Husn, in Northern Jordan

The tell rises like a mesa, wind-smoothed,
Above a village of concrete and brown stone -
Two state-run petrol pumps, red topped;
A row of hollow shops on the Jarash road,
A white, chipped police shed, two guards seated
Outside in back-tilted chairs, their gray-blue
British wools broken by silver stripes and badges,
Laughing, smoking, and sipping tea from glasses,
Watching the lorries labor by on their way
To Mafraq or Damascus, grinding gears, belching
Rich, oily spoor into the wind, past the bare
Hard hillside stacked with one-story poured
Cubes of concrete four meters square,
Mud-daubers' nests on a shelf in Judea,
The interstices here and there flapping
With the flags of pants and skirts, shirts
And scarves in livid pink and chartreuse,
As if to mock the hot, dry hills with color.

Al-Husn Camp: for forty years a cistern dry
Of hope, a stamp for landless feet, a station
For those who cannot go up or back,
For those orphans too knowing to rear,
Who are always no older than ten, who
Cross a border on the buttocks of a friend
Or clutch the bombs of a brother's dream;
There is no other way, it seems, to be
Other than someone everyone wants dead.
The boxes rest peaceably, scattered on the hill
Like magazines spilled from a munitions crate,
Waiting for the practiced hands, shouted
Orders, urgently whispered commands . . . .

Lina Elias Owais, Shahir Homoud, Qasim Koufali,
Hiyam Al-Nashash, Suhir Tarrar, Muhummed Abu-Gassim,
Skin thin as parchment, thin as promises,
Thin as waiting lists for passports, for change,
Skin stretched tight as the belly of an
Expectant cat, the lives squirming underneath,
Hungry for the light and air, for prey:
Bassam Iseed, Abdollah Bayeg, Ahlam Al-Madoun,
Waiting, thin-skinned, behind the tell
Whose worth in potsherds and broken tools
Archeologists from five countries
Are so eager to unearth.

# At the Pond's Edge

Down between a blackjack oak
And a hickory, a few dewberry
Vines scraping at my boots, down
Past the dollar weed and broom
Grass, topiaries all of a sylvan host,
I reach the liminality of worlds,
Where shore slides beneath the
Oily calm, the membrane of the
Living pond, secreting denizens
As my eyes, imbued with tinctures
Of sky, try to lever, to pry, a peening
Peening peening of a redbird holding
Fast, and a flushed frog plops a brief
Disturbance, water spiders hesitating
Then resuming their lazy circles in
The tension of boundaries. I assess
The bank for a swollen curve of
Cottonmouth, seeing none, intrude
A finger, and accept a limitation,
Ungratefully so.

# Dupuytren's Contracture

*Gloucester: O, let me kiss that hand.*
*Lear: Let me wipe it first; it smells of mortality.*

The sutures were all removed
A scant week after the surgery,
A lurid zigzag zipper of an incision
Made to scrape bound tendons clean
To release a thumb, my writing hand,
My dad come throw the football hand,
And it was all going very well, flexing,
Mending fast, but for a gape of pale lips,
A gash in the web that would not close,
Still slick and wet—and this morning
Brushing my teeth I smelt it out: decay,
Rot, infection between essential fingers,
Ones I made a living by, and I, reminded
That all too soon for who I am, the laden
Vessel of me would follow.  My little
Ones and ones I shared this scant sea
With will scent decay as one last
Memory of who I had been.

# Glouchester Cathedral

Cold thick stones, the floor still
Flecked with rushes, as if no mere
Thousand years had penetrated here,
The hard faces of tombs, of those lying
On their cases, chrysalises of marble
Facing upward, prepared even now to
Rise; and the walls, draped with once-
Crimsoned and azured banners now sere
As cobwebs, paintings dim as old sins
With the smoke from candles, the resin
Of incense, the residue of souls sweating
And rubbing and crying out and up for
Cleansing and hope and care, the souls
Of centuries thick in the air about me
In a supplication so self-sacrificial
As to impoverish the works of my hands,
The walls hold me as once my mother had,
When I had done wrong and knew, and
Knew there was still time to change.

# Malachite Beach
North Padre Island, Texas


As our children watched, I
Swept up clumps and bunches of
Sargasso weed one after another
And shook them like ringing bells
Into our bucket, the children's eyes
Waiting as at a gift's unwrapping, and
Down there tumbled out of the caramel
Brown branches, secreted amongst the
Tough and tiny leaves and salty berries
Delicate shrimp, some striped, some
Brown as dead grass, crabs all sandy
With white dots, some grey clay colored,
All with pinchers spread wide across the
Bucket's bottom, circling, fanning out
Like knife fighters in some Bodega's
Shadow after dark—and one terrified
Sergeant major, a frightened fish not
Long as my thumb, suspended, at last
Concealed as he might, under a sprig
Of seaweed carelessly tossed....The
Children watched and wondered and
Owned in their round world before,
With regret, relinquishing, agreeing
To let it all go back into the wash of
Waves into the gulf.

# Near the Suq

Amman, Jordan

"Marhabar," he had said, in greeting, and
I stepped down the worn steps at the end
Of an alleyway where shops selling anything
From charcoal brought in on donkeys to grey
Chickens steamed nearly soft in billowing vats,
Repaired aluminum pots to bolts of British wool
Spilled their wares into the concrete path, his
Dark shop advertised by neither sign nor lettering,
He and I and another expatriot teacher its only
Inhabitants here below the  sun-glared street,
Wandering from one alcove or dim corner to
Another, the shopkeeper sometimes drifting
Off to a nearby wall to snap a switch, illumining
Shelves of Bedouin coffee pots, lids and spouts
Curled or bent according to their tribe, blackened
In long-cold wadi encampments; brass Turkish
Coffee grinders, or the heavy wooden mortars,
Their pestles worn smooth of carving by years
Of oily hands working the blackened beans into
Powder at the approach of riders, beating a rhythm
Of warning or welcome, the now-dark holes almost
Conch shells to a listening ear; and I pawed through
Piles of felt kelims from the north, clattering selves
Of old cooking pots in battered copper, pots in
Cracked clay, "very old," he said, rolling his r's
Suggestively, and so I rattled and opened, turned
Over and rubbed, sniffed and shook my way over
This debris of a dying life, amassing an array of
Pots and broken hashish water pipes, one smallish
Clay jar, its mouth tightly sealed with a mud and
Straw stopper God knows when, two Bedouin
Tent rugs, and an old musket, its blackened stock
Studded in decorative nails, and the bargaining
Began, the merchants' theatre, "very very old,"
He said, "from underground," he mysteriously

Added, and I countered "ma-feesh," with gentle
Scorn, "broken," "real whool," he said, I, noting
A ravel, clicked my tongue and jutted a jaw, and
We at last wrestled to a price he insisted wrenched
Food from the mouths of his children, we sat, a boy
Brought tea, and we smoked cigarettes, satisfied,
And I rose to leave, telling him I hadn't enough
Dinars, about four hundred dollars, but would
Return from Irbid, where I lived, several hours'
Journey to the north, the following week; keep
Them for me, I conveyed, "la, la, la," no, no, he
Insisted, "take them now," he pushed, packed
Them for me and bundled me on my way, this
Man I had not met until that day. . . .

But as way does indeed lead on to way, and I
Found myself more than a month disabled and then
Immobile in Queen Alia's charity hospital far away,
That a story for another day, finally I returned to that
Shop I had so long left unrequited, a stiff back brace
Causing me to sidle in, finding the man at ease in the
Rear, like a sultan amidst his wealth; and as he rose
To greet, I embarrassed, smiling, extended my sheaf
Of brightly colored bills, spilled out my tale of woe
And said I knew he had worried where his money and
That Engleesi had gone, but, arm about my shoulder,
He said, solemnly, he had never been concerned,
Saying, "I knew what kind of man you are," and
Meant the words, shaming me for not believing in
His judgment, swelling and burdening me in this
World of ignorance and bliss.

# The Bat Room

Old Baines Place
Outside Hulett, Wyoming


We were just poking around, saw where some
Hunters had dressed out a few deer under the
Shelter of a tottering shed, looked into two
Immense cisterns underground, concrete-lined,
Looking like the pupils of sightless eyes, but
The images of dreams, too, and a room in the
Floor-buckled house, moldy books without
Shelves, more signs of dreams and minds seeing
A new world, a new home, come to mold and
Dust and decay, a pile of porcupine droppings
On the kitchen floor. And then out we went
Into a sun room, flat-roofed, jalousied windows,
Jalousies, of all things, tropical eyes batting
Delicate lashes against Wyoming blizzards and
Snow drifts house high....And from the barren
Rafters, inside the eaves, we saw the tiny and
Secret forms, heard the chee chee chee of brown
Bats, dozens of them back in the darkness from
That sunny day peering out; and central almost
As an apple tree a heavy post, hung with a pair
Of Carhardt coveralls drew me like a candle,
I, seeing the floor littered thick with guano gave
That suit a shake—and out flew more than two
Dozen bats, joined by some of their fellows from
The rafters, and my small children screamed and
Cried, my wife, too, and I scooped up Andrew
Terrified, I'm sure our sounds hideous and
Frightful to the ears of those creatures clearly
Hearing the drone of mosquitoes across a dark
Glade, this room filled with the confused chee
And flutter of bats, as I tried to hush us all, in
Wonder, saying stop, don't be afraid, look, they
Fly all around us, be still, they don't even touch
Us with their wings: the air was awash with tiny
Bodies—we stood amazed, transfixed, as they
Slowly subsided into eaves or fabric and at last
The room was still—not a one of them had
Touched us, but they did.

# The Monarchs,
on the way back


Thank God I am not too old
To stop for butterflies, as on
The flight path I found myself
Striding back to the office on
A crisp fall day—did the pair
Dipping and fluttering monarchs
Feel the stilettoed crystals of the
Keening year, for their flight was
More determined than my day,
And I saw another pair, higher
Still, and then several more, until
All my sky seemed filled with the
Stained-glass-window wings of
Monarchs moving south, driven
From unseen mountain meadows,
From child and flower-thronged
Backyards and milkweed vacant
Lots, joining their fellows in that
Quest for the fecund forests of old
Mexico, hundreds, thousands of
Miles away, to breed and die in
Unwavering purpose—the bliss
Of this world sometimes lifts,
Sometimes chides me in its
Inexorability.

# The Whistle Buoy

A blocked fuel line, a fallen breeze, and
I was behind, trying to make Dauphin Island
And an anchorage across a long and open stretch
Of shoaling sound, but down the sun dropped,
A luminous gold, a knowledge and an eye,
Before I made the shore.

Night drew its cloak tight around my shoulders,
Moonless, a glittering shower of stars overhead,
But a low mist and a hard chop, an old chart
Kept comfort out of reach, as I longed to
Drop the hook and rest.

Out of the deep mystery of the dark,
Under the sound of wind and waves
Was carried the low and calm hoooot
Of the whistle buoy, a long pause, and again
The sad refrain telling of wellhead or wreck,
The hoooot blowing slow and passionless
Out of the dense fabric of the dark,
Like some drowned corpse playing a bone flute,
The fleshless fingers touching the holes,
The ghost of a sailor blowing the notes,
Calling for company under the waves,
Calling me to my grave,
And I was afraid.

# Thoughts of Grape Soda and the Keys

One taste of grocery-brand grape soda, and
The taste of those plump crusty macaroons,
Too, floods back to me, those weekends in
The Florida Keys, drinking the Chek sodas,
Eating macaroons Dad got at the grocery near
The Snake Creek bridge, and I, alone, would
Linger, drop a crumb of macaroon into the
Bath-warm water, watch it slowly drift down
In the crystal, past a coral shelf, sometimes
A passing mojarra or sergeant major would
Snap it up, or it would fall almost to bottom
Less than a leg down before a green-spotted
Goby, like a two-inch grouper, would appear
And the crumb would vanish with a snap
And tiny cloud of disturbed sand—there
Was my world.

Sometimes I'd change my bobbered and
Baited snapper rig for a hook thin as a hair,
Pack a seed-pearl of macaroon on it and
Grab a mojarra or goby—never a sergeant
Major—hook it through the meat behind the
Dorsal with a larger hook, cast out, and wait
For a barracuda or something I had not yet
Caught. A small cuda went on a still larger
Hook and might thrash and glint his way to
The attention of larger jaws, always larger
Jaws, bigger fish....And where was Dad
When this world of mine was rolling on?
And what was he being? And I, seeing my
Sons making scrap-lumber forts or Lego
Towns, digging deep holes into our soft
Earth, where are they as I, excluded,
Watch?

# Through my eyes

"Pray without ceasing"—I Thessalonians 5:17

Praying with my eyes, through my eyes:
A morning sea mist, sun glaring, four
Brown pelicans swinging in formation
Over a rhythm of green waves, wing
Feathers skimming the water's surface
On the leeward side; red clover laden
With the diamonds of dew at first light;
And not just the flaming strokes of a
Clouded set of sun but the grim gradation
From periwinkle blue to the soft violet
Presaging night, the first bright star in
The east; the swollen gum of a toddler
Before the teeth emerge, deciduous;
The crimson gash of a sliced tomato
From the garden; an aqua and carmen
Hieroglyph under a lintel at Thebes
Three thousand years old, the coded
Hieroglyph on a blue crab's back, his
Claws the azure of a cold winter sky;
The lush shiny lobes of a spinach leaf:
All and each the sweep of creation,
My silent breath of thankfulness riding
Waves of light through oracles of iris
Into the depths of mind,
Without ceasing.

# Tony Mares

was born and raised in Albuquerque, New Mexico, educated in local schools, went on to university courses and completed a doctorate in European history. However, beginning in his early to mid-twenties, poetry became the real focus of his attention. Over the years, he  published several books of poetry and his poems have appeared in numerous venues.  He also has one book of translations of the poems of the Asturian poet, Ángel González.

# FALLEN ANGELS

There are only four statues to the devil in the world.
Three of them are in Spain, one in Italy (Turin).

I  EL ANGEL CAÍDO

(the fallen angel)

Bellver, the sculptor, caught him
With the horror etched on his face.
He had fallen for untold light years
Down the well of time and tragedy.

Bellver finally nailed him in 1885,
Cast him in bronze.  Gave him
A log to sit on and serpents
To cover his genitals.  Now he reigns
Atop a pedestal in the Retiro,

Madrid.  How fitting this angel
Of many names should end up
In a royal park, near the Prado
And streets leading to Plaza del Sol,

Madrid, the very heart of the city,
Where a bear, also bronze, greets
Tourists and revelers at dawn.
During those few, quiet moments
In the Retiro, the angel recalls
The crowds in 1936, leaves his pedestal,
And flies to Plaza del Sol.

He hovers like a fiery eagle,
A bird of prey exulting in the cries
"Viva la república! Viva la revolución!"
Franco, the fatted bishops,
The Fascists, and the Civil Guard

Soon replied with machineguns,
Bombs at Guernika, bodies covered
By screams, the delicious odors of flies,
And their own cry, 'Viva la muerte!"

The angel bides his time,
Trusting the good times to return.
Doesn't matter he is ignored.

How foolish the poet, coughing
His lungs out, walks by the Retiro,
Doesn't even see the Fallen Angel.


## II EL ÁNGEL CAÍDO DE SANTA CRUZ DE TENERIFE.

Look away fallen angel and flee.
Let your menacing wings take you
Far away from this island in the sea.

Canary Islands, the City of Santa Cruz de Tenerife.
A fallen angel greets you at the Military Museum.
Only he didn't used to be so fallen. Juan de Ávalos
Sculpted him in 1966. Ah, but that was then.

The angel looks like a stealth bomber, or a drone,
Ready to strike like invisible lightening and thunder.
Above him, a man, maybe a priest, who looks like Franco,
Leans on a sword as he rides the angel on to . . . what?
New victories for "One, Great, and Free" Spain?

Everyone calls it the "monument to Franco."
Same sculpture, after Franco's death, but now called
"Monument to the Victory," or "Monument to His Excellency,
The Chief of State." A coy Foundation now calls it
"The Monument to Peace." But the government of Tenerife
Changed the name to "Monument to the Fallen Angel."

So what is he? Fallen angel? Sinister angel who looks
Like a dive bomber? Fascist angel? All of the above.

Angel Caído, rise on your bomber wings, flee
This lovely island in the sea.

A chihuahua walks by, lifts its leg, gives his opinion
Of the angel, with a fine golden stream.


## III THE FALLEN ANGEL OF THE FREGUS TUNNEL

He is the laid-back angel
Standing on a pyramid of rocks
Miners dug from the tunnel between France and Italy.
Back in 1879, this kind of statue paid high tribute
To our real gods, Science and Technology.

He is the laid-back angel casting light
on the miners who died excavating the tunnel.
Like titans, their pale bodies scattered
Around the angel's pedestal. Yet that light
Comes from a star stuck clumsily
Into the angel's head. Otherwise, you'd never know
He was the very devil himself, Lucifer,
The light bearer, saying, "I'm the new god,
This is the new path to salvation."

Yet he is such a laid-back angel. Looks
Out of shape. Flabby muscles. Marcello,
The sculptor, or to give his imposing name,
Marcello Conte Panissera de Veglio,
With a name like that, maybe he wanted
A laid-back angel, boring but reliable.

Still, despite the stupid star on his head,
He just really can't be Lucifer.


## IV EL ÁNGEL EXTERMINADOR

The Exterminating Angel hovers above
Comillas, looking out to the Atlantic

From the Cantabrian coast.
Such a beautiful site for an angel in 1895,
Even a fierce one, to spend his time!
Josep Llimona, modernist that he was,
Sculpted the angel above a cemetery,
Itself above the ruins of an ancient church.

Hard to believe the Book of the Apocalypse
Calls this angel the "Angel of the Bottomless
Pit," who does not bear "the stamp of God
On his forehead." He's supposed to reign
Over plagues of locusts that will devastate
All of us. Well, the locusts are already here,

But this angel deserves better. He is peaceful,
Almost abandoned in this small village
By the Atlantic coast. Pigeons
Show him no respect and he is covered
In their disdainful droppings.
He deserves better. His other name,
Guardian Angel, makes him more at home
Here, as he keeps watch over the fallen
Walls and imploded dreams of an old church,
The architecture of vacant-eyed skulls
And blinding white bones.

# At Concordia Cemetery, El Paso

(in memory of my daughter Galit)


At Concordia Cemetery, El Paso,
near John Wesley Harding's grave
and the Baptist Reverend Reed's,
I think of you.  A butterfly

flutters its wings. That small effect
makes an unpredictable wave,
weathers the world and drives a straw
through a tree or sways the sunflower

bending to the pressure of the sun.
You were, you are, that impulse,
a zigzag flight to your own beat
across the stars. The Chinese

on the other side of a dividing wall
sleep beneath their stately stones.
Gunslinger, preacher, the Chinese
tell their tales to the common loam.

I hear no song in the border sky.
Silence sings where you have been.
I try to remember your voice
and I hear the chorus of the wind.

# Hilbert's Hotel

We were an enormous horde
come out of the void to become
alpha naught, invincible numbers
stretching forever to infinity.

Our advance guard came to the hotel,
demanded rooms, tamales, drinks for all.
"My hotel is infinitely full," Hilbert
the owner said. "But I'll tell you
what I can undo.  Give me a minute."

He moved guest number one to suite two
and guest number two to suite four.
All the even numbers filled but the odds
became infinitely empty.

Our horde moved in.  We drank all the wine,
ate all the tamales.  We terrorized
the even-numbered bros.
"Don't provoke them," Hilbert said.
"They are as many  as you."

We sang the sad corridos,
offered chicharron burritos
to our even-numbered bros.
The party didn't last.
Fights broke out.
Even among numbers
things get irrational.

*David Hilbert (1862-1943), a German mathematician, illustrated
the concept of infinity with his famous "hotel," which could be infinitely
full, yet infinitely empty.*

# I Carry Neruda in My Backpack

Pablo Neruda
is a thick volume
in my backpack.
He is many pounds of poems.

As I walk along the street,
I step on gravel that replies,
surprised, in a crunchy kind of voice,
—It's Neruda —
small shoots of grasses
that dare to rise up
through the cracks in the sidewalk
sigh — Neruda —

There's an aroma of spring,
of renovation, in the air.
The squealing tires say —
the pavement on Central Avenue
will crumble and a new world
sprout from these ruins
because Neruda came through here —

And suddenly comes running,
and running, running, up the street,
heading east, in a big hurry,
the pink pig Neruda lifted
to poetry. The pig hurries
to meet the new-born sun
for he carries on his skin
the color of the dawn.

# Otowi Bridge

You see the swift current here
and know there is white water
all the way down to Cochiti dam
twenty four miles away.

You've crossed the Rio Grande
at the Otowi Bridge.
Look to your right and you'll see
Edith Warner sitting there.
Tilano, as always, is at her side.

Edith is all smiles and good cheer,
tea and cakes for visitors.
Tilano is reserved, gentle,
a San Ildefonso elder.

What must he think when the man
in the porkpie hat, a pipe
eternally in his thin lips,
comes down from Los Alamos
with Niels Bohr to visit with Edith?
Oppie, they call him, and Niels,
two philosopher scientists
who reflect on the jitterbug

of fast particles
in the quantum world.

You wonder if Tilano sees
inside these scientists' brains
a dark metal, compressed
to desperation, about to burst
into unforgiving mushrooms
of light?

You'll never know.
In the morning glory sky
the sun hovers in deep blue
above this gap where the river
falls away to the south.

# Rio Grande Rift

Beneath the heaving land
tectonic plates grind
like angry teeth. The earth
opens and spews out
mountains and volcanoes
all along the rift.

Before our kind appear,
insects, from the pallid wind scorpion
to the monarch butterfly,
spread over the land.
Birds, from the great blue heron
to the red-tailed hawk
fly and circle above the river.
Shrews, bats, rabbits, squirrels
of all description abound.
Always hunting, or hunted,
foxes, coyotes, black bears,
bobcats and mountain lions
move along the rift.

Rain pours down the slopes
and volcanoes of the Jemez
Mountains, gathers into streams,
the swift flowing arroyos.
The Rio Grande becomes
a wide, powerful river, then recedes
in the late summer
along the rift.

Before our kind appear.

# Meditation

Sheets of fire rise, rain down
From long fissures in the earth,
Fifteen hundred centuries ago.

Lava pushes up through earth's crust,
Flows to form the West Mesa.
Five volcanoes freeze
Along the western horizon.

Long before Albuquerque,
Our caves and campsites
Grow into villages,
Stumble into cities,
Leap into dreams, nightmares.

Carvers of petroglyphs leave silent
Images on the basalt rocks.
They speak of the quiet world,
Clean air, clear streams,
The movement of deer, fox,
Mountain lion across the landscape.

Five volcanoes are still here,
The land, the space, belong
To you, to me, to all creatures.
In the slow carvings of space and time,
Five volcanoes keep watch,
Their rings of fire carefully hidden
Under a mantel of lava fields.

I walk every day into the past
Become future. A cool breeze,
The sky, sun, point the way
Out of this choking, snarling now.

# North of the Central Avenue Bridge

(thinking of Galit)


North of the Central Avenue Bridge,
along the river's edge, trails cut
through thick undergrowth. Grama grass,
cholla, chamisa, goatheads, little blue stem
gather around cottonwoods felled by beaver.

It is late winter, the first days of March.
The river is still cold from snow melt
filtering down the Rio Grande rift
from the Jemez and the Sangre de Cristos.

Where the river flows around a snag of pine,
cottonwood and thistle, a kingfisher perched
on a scraggly branch waits to dive for trout.

Mallards in nervous flight, their sleek bodies
far forward of the thrashing wings, circle once,
swoop down near the undercut left bank.

For hours, the sandhill cranes wheel and turn,
winging north in majestic V's
towards their summer wetlands home.

Somewhere the whine of an electric saw,
the shout of a child and the monotone of traffic
on the Central Avenue Bridge
rise like a symphony to the coming spring.

Just once on a day exactly like this,
I wanted to walk the river bank with you,
to answer your questions about cranes
and about where the river comes from.

Daughter, I am undone by your absence.
All questions and answers dissolve
in a great haloing of wings overhead.
The sandhill cranes circling the sun.

# On John Conway's "Game of Life"

Imagine a life
without blinkers oscillating on off on off
or gliders inching down the diagonal line
like pixel snails groping toward infinity

Imagine a life
where you die of loneliness
but come back to life if three neighbors
stunned by your absence
bring you back because it's a rule
you can't die like that

Imagine a life
where your daughter never dies
or if she dies she's only turned off
for a while and will be on again before sunset

Imagine a life
where you might reach a steady state
like a traffic light or become a still life
a barge anchored in a calm bay
an abandoned beehive subject only
to the whims of the wind
reflected in a silent pond

Imagine a life
where death is abstract
and only symbols stop breathing
Imagine that

# Shadow Geometry

Balloon Festival time and
I read Einstein in cold morning light
on the geometry of shadows.

A sphere, a balloon, he says,
casts a shadow on a plane surface.
He's trying to explain space-time curvature,
multi-dimensional objects
to the math illiterate.

A great balloon, like a gift from Einstein,
floats south in the October sky,
cuts the light streaming from the sun,

casts a flat shadow on the wall.
Einstein smiles from the page,
winks at me, waves goodbye.

# Wings

Hummingbird, colibrí, tzintzun,
the word I prefer, for its
message of 'here now, moving
fast, gone with a low Doppler moan.'

Little guy, that tzintzun, has the movements
of a boxer, only bird who can fly
backwards with grace
unlike certain politicians but
I won't go there.

For now
enjoy the buzz-blurr
of wings buoyant,
the sky a whirl of blue and vectors
open to the future.  El tzintzun
breaks our bonds of gravity
lifts us out of ourselves
for an eternity in its tiny head.

# Ronald E. Moore

was a health care executive for thirty years. He has a BA in Philosophy and an MBA in Finance from TCU. He is a composer, adventurer (103 countries) human rights activist, with a strong interest in Tibetan freedom. He has one book of poetry, *Alterity* (Current Press) and has been published in *descant* and other venues. He has two sons and lives in Fort Worth, Texas.

# Metaphysics in the Park

There was little indication
that the man on the bench
was doing metaphysics in the park,
(though he did know the number
of photons in his body: 10 times 27 zeroes),
felt hat, Sunday Times,
inappropriate overcoat in spring.

He was imagining dark energy moving through his body,
whose atoms had always been somewhere,
since time began,
before being gathered in him—
in a subterranean rock on Mars,
the tail of a cheetah,
in the laurel wreath Aurelius accepted from the Mystery cults of Eleussis.

He saw in the eternal wind:
a serpentine of Russian poets, their right hands crushed,
a tablet saying: *the lies of a government are worse than a thousand broken hearts,*
a tent flap loose, dangling,
the hallowed laughter of a female child,
the mouth of hell that swallowed Jews and Gypsies,
an alabaster statue of Athena.

Carrying within him these too many worlds—
carved out his loneliness,
inscribed him, a hologram, in time.

## The Real Funeral

When the suits and the dresses and the preachers went away,
we had the real funeral, my brother and I sitting in the gravel
of a town we'd shaken off long ago.

We got there just as Fatboy and his gravedigger friends
were finishing their job. They were sweeping around their
newest grave, the place that was our father's last one.

They didn't seem surprised that we came back.
One man drove by and said, "Your daddy was a good one,"
but quickly had the sense to go away.

In the silence made heavy by our grief, my brother finally said,
"Dad, I'm gay." I said, "Mother, I didn't love you, but you
had my respect," two long-suppressed benedictions.

We wondered aloud how far apart they were, so Fatboy
got a measure, told us twenty-one inches. It seemed about right.
The gravel and the grave and Fatboy in a small Georgia town.

When they were ready to leave, Fatboy turned to tell us,
"Think of it like putting a coat in the closet."
It was the best thing anybody said that day.

We stayed until we both felt calm begin to spread,
then we walked toward the useless, emptying house.
That was the way we closed the door.

# A Kind of Marriage

It's more than the touching—
the body's vernacular—
it's the seamless consonance,
a plaiting that insinuates
the entire layer of my dreams,
an integrity of wanting,
wanton in conspiracy—
who else could sense my fingers,
your breath still fresh upon them,
tapping out the rhythm of my poems
on your hip
while you sleep
after love.

# A Short History of Life

There was no love,
no race of Gods,
no music of any kind, faint or ephemeral.
Till molybdenum
riding on an asteroid
collided with a petri dish of cosmic drizzle—
a flask of gurgling gases—
on earth, life stirred.
Time wound its clocks, marked its calendars.

Beetles and seed spores
filled the floor of forests,
killer whales and fiddler crabs occupied the seas.
In far pastures ibex and catamount,
chrysanthemum, mossy marigolds,
the skies flecked with falcons and whippoorwills.
Then reasoning creatures—
bushmen striding out of Africa—
gathered at the rivers of the earth, its valleys, plains.

Nightfire tales were told,
paintings on cave walls and vases,
fear and wonder, singing their incomprehension.
Predators, disease, ghastly wars,
there was compassion, hunger,
mothers bringing babies to their bare breasts.
There was joy, brilliance,
increasing mastery of earth.
And under a single bulb in many dim rooms—
longing.

# A Giacometti Man

When he takes away
sufficiencies of clay,
the piece begins
to be finished.
Beauty, for him,
was to diminish,
inferring an inner form—
one which is found
by pounding off
the superfluous—
leaving the fibrous core,
then one cut more.
As were fond portions
of me culled by the
long spanned hand
of choice, time
and circumstance.

# The Importance of Metaphor

The most accurate description of bread
    is hunger.
The most incisive depiction of water
    is thirst.

If you haven't experienced hunger or thirst,
    I could write two hundred poems about love
    and you wouldn't comprehend it.

Bleak man became human using metaphor,
    the snow leopard appeared out of snow,
    the giraffe from the higher sweeter leaves.

Mathematics is a language we employ
    to better understand and rule our world,
    by analogy,
    by guile.

## Passion

The morning after the first time together,
I found a note folded by the orange juice.
"Don't tell me you love me if you don't."
        She was Cuban.
        Among other things,
        her passion was pure tobacco leaf,
        fragrant smoke, incendiary eyes.
        Her father was a famous freedom fighter,
        who either did or didn't
        hide on a bridge,
        attack by himself a Cuban boat.
I was scrupulously careful in everything I said after that.

# Kotor

The shanked up slabs of
mountain, black,
cup the deep water like a chalice,
from which the hills drink their
greenness, their gold, their glimmering.
Against the cliff,
a white numinous wall.
In the upper left a medieval window.
A lingering impression,
that were the glass open
you could find a burnished secret
nested behind the stolid wall.
But the hasp on the window frame is broken,
it won't budge.
Oblivious to questions,
a boy wastes a lazy afternoon,
throwing a ball against the wall.
It comes back each time,
true, catchable, mute.

## False Premises

It was 1812. The boy who first
saw the dusty cloud was only nine.
Bravery flared, he ran through
Riga crying that the army was
only miles away. Resolutely,
citizens burned their buildings,
all seven hundred-forty, and their
farmlands, depriving Napoleon
of all their worldly goods. Of
such heroism history is comprised.
What arrived was a thundering
herd of hungry cattle. The Emperor
was elsewhere plundering.

## On the Standards and Terms
## By Which Certain Words
## Are Described as Poetry

Language,
in a pensive interlude,
rises from its studious,
well stuffed chair,
puts one foot forward
in its worn, polished shoe,
then the other—
and hearing an esoteric music—
starts dancing,
the movements
gradually,
accumulating grace.

# Accidental Happiness

I am not smarter than to write
   fragile hopes on the vellum of despair.
Like a cedar-waxwing drunk on
   laurel cherry leaves,
I've always stumbled into
   accidental happiness.

Rode out against feckless
   hate. Dreamed another planet's
Jewelry. Made a coat of many
   colors from a hair shirt. Foraged
For love on the plain of disasters,
   put on the skin of all the earth.

In fact, I've assembled
   the city of a convoluted joy—
And now, body slowing, the
   soul avoiding corrosion so far—
Am still fiercely grinning at its
   gradual, reluctant relinquishing.

# The Warrior's Trajectory

Scurrilous, the slaughter of innocents,
Respecting the life and death of only their own.
But the Vikings got this part of it right—
Put the body on a well-carved boat.
Drape it on a bed of rare sandalwood.
In his hand place the thing he loved most.
At sunset, on a still, somber day,
Push the boat from the shore.
Loose flaming arrows into the wood.
Stand in hawk-like honor while it burns.
Watch while the boat goes, slowly,
Where it's going.

# The Reprieve

Three angels took me roughly to the patio.
Lit three candles, did not offer wine.
The ugly one snorted— your report?
Two sons, ex-wife, a career, no
crimes, many books, a little poetry.
We know that the dark one retorted—
but what was the fulcrum of your life?
I have been broken only by love
and wonderment. And I know
almost nothing for certain.
The beautiful one rose, indicated
their departure, spoke softly cross her
languorous shoulder— your answer
was sufficient and amusing,
we grant you a little more time.

# The Soft Parade

I have been struck silent
by the stacked up,
pressed together beauty
of the Sistine Chapel.
Was followed in the Prado by
Velasquez's painted eyes,
wherever in the hall I stood.
But I remember most—
the fluttering fall of her dress,
the soft parade
of her bare feet walking
toward me.

# I See the Humor of It Now

She could have made a fool
out of Solomon, Diogenes and Kant,
all in one day. She was that—

goddess— remarkable. Canaletto
would have laid down his brush
on the spot. And I was in a line

I didn't know the length of,
greedy for the excess, the mad
extravagance, as if I'd

wandered in a cave, found
grouchy old Catullus,
scribbling on his parchment,

and he handed me a note which said,
"The love of a beautiful woman
is more than the conquering of Spain."

But a poet's lines were useless,
in light of her capricious disappearing.
I'll be bold and tell you: my heart,

once ravaged, is now cleaned out,
a place so empty,
the universe itself couldn't fill it.

# Karla K. Morton

the 2010 Texas Poet Laureate, is a member of the Texas Institute of Letters and graduate of Texas A&M University. Described as "one of the most adventurous voices in American poetry," she is a Betsy Colquitt Award Winner, *twice* an Indie National Book Award Winner, and the author of seven books of poetry.

# Becoming the Father You Always Wanted

This is for all the sons
with the wounds from their fathers
still gaping in their chests –
words, like cigar burns,
on the inside of their ribs,
hived up; unhealing.

For you who sat, crying in the dark
so no one would see;
mother watching from the kitchen,
hands wringing in the dishtowel

as you curved over your knees
like the crescent moon,
waiting for the one who never came.

Or you who begged for a game of catch,
though vodka stumbled his legs;
living with the guilt of hating him –
as all teenagers hate;

then losing him early — before you could learn
to love him as a man.
This is your clay, your darkness, your pain.

But let me tell you, there is tenderness
inside your fists;
and the stone wall of your heart
is worn smooth by my body
crossing over in the moonlight;

and that man who came before you —
that nine kinds of son-of-a-bitch;
that volcano spewing molten lava

gave you the very earth you stand on,
and these moments of pause —

when you raise your sons
like crystal goblets to the sky,
your hands, never once,
letting go.

# Palindrome

*Palindrome — a word, line, verse, number, etc, reading the same backward as forward.*

Today, I am learning to be *Dog* —
waking when my bladder rumbles,
or when I thirst, or hear footsteps,
or when the blue sky is too irresistible to wait.

I have to go out now.

I want to nose and bless
each tire and tree;
feel unfiltered frenzy over squirrels;
give in to *every* temptation.

And I shall sit when I pause,
executing the perfect *Down Dog*,
and stare
and sniff the wind;

not worrying once
about the dog shit back home
on the carpet.

Because what matters most
are those french fries on your plate,
and the sun on my fur —

feeling a peace
that stretches every hour into seven;

a holiness that makes me think,
each time you say the word *God*,
that you are, somehow,
calling my name.

# Death at the Gorge

There had *only* been enough time
to call the police;
someone with binoculars
spotting the horrifying view —
a body splayed across the rocks
at the bottom of the Gorge.

He *had* to have come this way;
felt this perfect March day.
He would have seen the mountains
turning purple around him;
Earth giving *everything* she had to give;
yet he jumped anyway.

Hawks were circling;
five curly-horned rams
clogged their way along the ridge;
the river, roiled past.

And I stood, stunned,
with no answers for my children;
no comfort to give;
shocked life could barrel on
when he decided he could not.

If only he had turned *left* at the stoplight
instead of right.
He would have driven into Taos Valley;
had the best schnitzel and dark beer of his life;
sat beside the cool meander of the river;
his eyes only looking upward...

Maybe he would have ordered a second beer,
instead of lifting one leg,
then the other,
briefly grasping that silver rail behind him;
leaving the wind;
the world;
alone and gasping in his wake.

# Rhythm

A mouthful of saltwater and gagging,
I surfaced next to a pelican
laughing at this amateur
floundering to find the sync
of water and flow and breath
and awkward limbs.

And I'm 14 again,
an odd French Horn in my hands,
a foreign language of notes
on the page
*I will never figure out*;

the back of my eyes burning
as the others followed along
in their smooth current
of comprehension...

till the long 'C',
when in frustration,
I blew, and captured it —
that blessed note,
as round and full as the moon;

and the stroke of fingers understood
and the lungs held their air,
and rhythm rose on its dark wings,
wet and heavy from the sea.

# Ocean

I came to her, after her fevered night
expelling entrails of seaweed
and blue veins of glossy jellies,

to find her calm as a lullaby this morning;
waves purring back and forth at my feet.

Every day she is different —
her colour, her sound;
moods swelling with the moon —
this quintessential feline...

No wonder men named their ships women;
carved busty figureheads on the front —
trying to soothe ancient female mysteries
glazed tight as the pearls on her skin...

Feel how they hold her warmth
as she curls around you in the dark;
this descendant of the Sirens

one last breath in,
then you're hers.

# The E Ticket

*The Hospice House*

The room starts to get stuffy,
the oxygen machine —
white noise against the shuffle;
whispers and giggles
of gathering angels —
wings tucked like hearts at their backs.

Others arrive
as an odd anxiousness balloons;
six beds in queue,
waiting like portals
to whisk them into the next life;

rectangular roller coasters
into the unknown.

One room over,
someone's ride has begun.
Hear them all —
hands up and screaming.

## Tree Blossoms

March winds snow petals
with each gust;
white jewels in my hair, my tea.

Twelve years of drought
have brought her here —
tiptoe roots stretching deep

into hidden waters;
kinking garden hoses
to trickle in the night;

pouring every extra cup of ice
and bathwater at her feet
to make it through till Spring,

when tornados, like swirling demons,
try to crack her trunk;
sever her limbs...

Torturous storms beget each blossom;
there is hunger and burden and need;
don't think beauty easy.

# Persephone, the Bear

A 911 call about a bear in a kitchen,
and the firemen dispatched,
setting a trap with peanut butter...
and there she was.

It was the closest I'd ever been
to a bear— her gentle brown eyes
and triangle head;
her massive claws.

A summer of drought and fires
brought her down,
this goddess of Spring,
lured by hummingbird feeders

and dog food,
and a bowl of pomegranates
on the other side
of that cabin door.

It was protocol —
a trespassing bear was caught,
tranquilized and tagged,
then taken out to the wilderness

and inflicted with fear —
what the firemen dreaded —
yelling, throwing sand bags,
branches, stones,

firing shotguns; revving chainsaws;
then releasing trained bear dogs
to chase her back,
up into the mountain,

hopefully to never return;
knowing if they failed,
and *Brown Bear 377*
with the yellow ear tag

was caught again,
she would be killed…
the blood still fresh in the cage
from the last captive.

Ah, let the angels comfort her,
help her to forget the crunchy,
the salt and the sweet
of the underworld;

let her live to tell great grand-bears
about the cruel devils down there;
their lusty, forbidden foods;
those horrible, hellish hounds.

# Motel

Some may think I've lost my way,
calling this a place of ill repute —
human beings coming together,
a touch of lightning;
a transformation of two
becoming one.

Sometimes the soul needs
a little tango.

Thin sheets pulled up, hair tussled;
sharing chicken salad on beer bread
and a pluot from a paper sack;
the juice on your chin,
a siren's song; a plunge into your depths...
and I'm lost again;

the forsaken fruit, half-eaten on the nightstand;
its jeweled heart, exposed.

# Asphodels

I wonder, since you've gone,
if you can come and go when you want;
if you ever go back and visit that asphalt spot
where you left your body;
your spirit rising like the changing lights —
from yellow, to red, to green.

When I cross that street,
are you sometimes standing there?
Do I pass through you
like a sliver of rainbow?

Remember when our neighbour
died in his kitchen — how the dogs
would *never* go in there again?

But I don't mind.
I rather like the thought of you near.

Sometimes I sit at the window
when the sun slants in,
just to glimpse those iridescent flecks
that swirl and puddle
in the corners and cracks;

and it somehow moves me
when I see green stems thrusting up
from sidewalks or roadways —

too vibrant for the underworld;
unwilling to be contained;
refusing their allotted plots of darkness.

*Asphodels - the food of the dead that grows on the surface*
*but whose roots go down to the underworld.*

## Silence

Earth fills the silence with all things growing.
We sit by the creek; our ears full of creeping thyme,
and blossoms,

and sinking rain. The deep breathing of the oaks,
inhaling our worries, blurring the distinction
between heaven

and earth. See how we burst, like squirrel-deep,
sprouting walnuts! Life is no greater than one
perfect moment.

I hear you, my Beloved, in thick honeysuckle
winds; my heart reaching for you, like the slow
green curl of a fern.

# Sign Language

*for Ed Patton*

His was a generation
that nearly outlasted the
next — burying
all but two of his seven girls before
he turned 90.

Years ago, with no hopes of
an heir for his fields, he sold
that Chico farm,
took up wildcatting; the untimely swing
of chain against

spinning steel, dropping fingers,
one by one, into oil black
holes — a part of
him buried first, like it should be — one for
every daughter.

# Roundness of the World

There's a *rage for order on the plains*,
an order I cannot understand.

The mockingbird dives for the junebug;
the butterfly;
bobcats break tiny chipmunk backs;
coyotes cull lame-legged  lambs.

There is a wisdom here
beyond my frail emotions—
my instinct to save the deer
from the lion; to deny
baby rattlers the rabbit.

And in the drought,
when the little red calf
I dared to name
stumbled, then fell,

only God could have looked upon
the feast of the vultures,
and declared,
without doubt,
*it is good.*

# One Night In Florida

I want to tell you something I've tried to say for 23 years;
about one night on the Ft. Pierce Inlet,
in a 17-foot sailboat;

how youth and bluster and braying music
finally yielded to a silence
as rich and deep as the blackberry sky,
with only the slap of current against the curved bow;

how I spied a dolphin alongside the boat.

I want to tell you how he looked silver in the moonlight;
how I reached over the side, near the surface of the water;
how he rose to my palm, letting me stroke his long, slick back
again and again, each time he surfaced.

I want to tell you that after he swam away,
I held my hand up, in the dark,
and looked at it,
as if it had changed;

and how, from that day forward,
I have never lived an ordinary life.

# Elizabeth Raby

is the author of three full-length poetry collections and four chapbooks. Her poems have been translated into Romanian and she is co-author of a Romanian/English chapbook, *Oase, Carne, & Blana* *(Bone, Flesh & Fur.)* Winner of the 2010 Elmer Kelton Award, Angelo State University, she has been nominated several times for the Pushcart. A graduate of Vassar College (B.A.) and Temple University (M.A., Creative Writing), Ms. Raby has lived in Santa Fe, NM since 2000.

## A Moment

Standing outside at dusk in a heavy
wet April snowstorm, the door open
behind me, a Corelli violin concerto
pouring out over us all,
the weighted junipers,
the beauty bush's bending arms,
the hollyhocks' snow-filled cupped leaves,
the birds all silent and disappeared,
the daffodil, its face and yellow-fringed bonnet
pressed into the snow.
Suddenly I'm the small child afraid
that I too may break into pieces
under the pressure of so much beauty.

# Mrs. Hunt across the Street

A teacher once
before she was lost
to sadness, left alone
in its grasp, but she still loved
language and for awhile
was well enough
to share it with a little girl,
story after story,
day after day,
from the precious collection
first read to her son
so many years before.

Each morning she would bend
to the bottom shelf
of her glass-fronted bookcase,
select one from the row
of red leather-bound books,
the crackly paper gilt-edged,
to read to me
of a mermaid, dancing princesses,
wolves, houses on legs, a hen,
until depression's chokehold
silenced her again.

A ghost for so many years now
and in my memory, elusive,
a beautiful wisp I don't want to lose.

## At the Door

A splinter in the paw,
the wolf stops its stalk,
its scratch at the window,
lies down in the snow,
snuffles and nips.

In the quiet before
the cloudy mirror,
she braids her
long gray locks,
caresses her once
soft face, fingers
carved dry lines.
Meager soup
on the fire, watery
lentils and the last
bone of the lamb.

So empty—she
is tempted to open
the door, call in
the wolf. If he will
let her, she will urge
him to lie down
on the hearth, she will
pull out his thorn,
she will stretch out
beside him. Perhaps
she is almost ready—
if he eats her, better
than this long slow
loneliness. A few quick
bites, the flow of blood
to show she has been alive.
She would be somebody's
meal, somebody's
satisfaction.

# Bride-to-Be

Walking alone as she likes best,
beside dried mullein, its seed heads
open, old burrs bent double by the weight
of snow, she is startled by a dead root
reclining like a body with legs spread,
one knee bent, crack of vagina, chest
open, heart torn out, a single staring eye.
There one ant, more vigorous than she
will ever be, searches the small debris
of pine needles, tiny twigs, bits of dirt,
fallen into the broken wood.

She watches stellar jays, blue as the glass rods
that curtained the Temple of Heaven,
move in courtship climb up sun-spackled
vanilla-scented ponderosa pine. A pair
of tiny bushtits touch beaks on a slender
branch above juicy new sedum, spikes
of chive in bud. Here in brisk welcome
every dead stalk is fringed in green.

She begins a long climb past red
shoots of peonies, birches leaking sap,
until she reaches the peak at last.
Sunset colors melting snow violet red.
For now, she is replete, but tomorrow
she will leave behind these solitary
explorations, everything she knows.
She doesn't want to be opened and split,
a character in a man's life: She is afraid
to be tugged out of herself by a child.
If she could just remain here watching
geese fly toward the waxing moon.

# I Can't Remember Anymore

Was my father born in 1905—
my mother in 1907? And my
father's birthday—December 3rd
perhaps? And Mother's, August
something. Such a different world
they knew—little towns in dusty
Nebraska. My mother, the preacher's
kid, always under disapproving eyes;
my father, the banker's son, could
get away with anything. There was
the time he and his buddies pulled
someone's old milk cow up the steps
of the church steeple and tied her tail
to the bell rope—these days prison
time for sure, then a prank, although
my father did get a hiding. He soon
became the solid serious man I knew.
Mother's diary a revelation—in high school
she liked clothes, movies, expeditions
in the rich boy's car—all the things
she thought weren't necessary for me.

I would love to spend one day
watching them in their young lives.

## Sufficient

"About as well as can be expected considering
the material you have to work with."

All dressed up for the prom, a day of bathing,
plucking, curling, oiling, painting, corseting
behind me, the words a devastation at the time,
lurking in the mind an embarrassing number of years.

"Good enough that you won't be held back
by your appearance." Now grateful
to be navigating, more or less
healthy, more or less acquiescent
to the sags and blotches of time, I've come
to know there was wisdom in her words.

Not expecting to be anyone's object
of desire, "good enough" can be useful
to a woman. She doesn't have to be afraid
of the mirror—it was never her special friend.
While beauty can be frozen in a gaze,
the ordinary one is free to move about
unmolested, un-pursued. There is a lot
of space at the back of the room.

# e = (90% m + 10% b)

Let m stand for matter, b for bacteria, e for Elizabeth

Will my 10% bacteria die
when I do? Perhaps they slipped
from Mother to me by way
of the placental cord,
having already squirmed
through the long sea voyages
inside my English Quaker,
Swedish farmer ancestors.
Or perhaps they are my very own
explorers, warriors, enemies, allies
in the isolated island nation of my body.
How many, beneficial or malignant,
have I bequeathed to my children?

It may be our small colonizers
have traveled the whole world
divided as it is by culture and country,
by food and climate, to give us
something real to share.
Bacteria carried in common
by Samoans, Norwegians,
the Rom, the Sami, and me.

Survivors of plague, polio, flu, scourges
that ended so many lives and lines,
we travel in unknowing conspiracy,
boarded, held for ransom, by our tiny pirates.
At any moment violence may break out.

# A Poster—"Celebrate Women in the Arts"

In the art of the white petticoat
below the embroidered skirt,
with raised arms, turn and turn
and turn again,
fill your  baskets
with scabby apples,
hold them high above your head,
in the art of peeling each apple
in one long strip,
of coring and slicing and sprinkling
with lemon, the art
of rolling out pastry, of grating sugar
and grinding cinnamon,
lighting the wood in the oven,
building up a good fire,
of tamping it down
to the perfect temperature,
setting the pie to cool on the window sill,
of being patient with the man
who gobbles it down without so much
as a grunt of approval.

# White-Winged Dove

What does she think
as she walks a zigzag path
pursued by her puffed-up
pompous would-be mate?
He manages to keep in touch,
his beak to her tail,
losing dignity with every
graceless step.
She may not have
a sense of humor,
but I find myself
chuckling
as he slowly deflates.

# Glass

The liquid lies down,
pulled and folded in stripes,
blue water, white waves
gradually frozen
in the shape of forever,
but it is fragile,
can splinter back into fragments
almost like the sand it came from,
useful in its first form, beautiful
in its every form.

How did they know,
those Mesopotamians,
out of what lightning strike,
great fire, what burning settlement,
what time of peace
around a festival pyre,
did the first translucent drop appear?
For those who tried and tried
to extend and shape that miracle,
tried and, no doubt, failed,
tried and failed and tried again:
the world a vessel humans
can shatter, still, persisting,
we gather the shards.

## *Cetate* (Fortress) Deva, Romania

A small stone monument stands behind
an iron gate beneath the curved brick
of the otherwise empty dungeon.
*Here David Ferenc the founder*
*of the Unitarian Church was martyred*
*in the prison of this castle, 1579.*

Outside, the courtyard is littered
with bits of stone, ragweed, plastic,
cigarette butts, crumbling bricks.
A painted blue peace sign fades
on gray stone, names are scratched
on broken walls.

Something white protrudes from packed
earth. She picks it up before she recognizes
a tooth, the enamel perfect, the root unscarred,
wrenched from some young human mouth.

All around the exhalation of souls
slips past in the air above her, touches
her skin, gently entreats her to know them,
to ask what happened here and why.

The atoms of the anonymous mingle
with those who kept them so, who wanted
them to remain polite in their graves, in their
blowing ash, their stories and their anguish
lost. Still they whisper and nudge, a quiet
disturbance of the atmosphere.

# Sightseeing in Romania

On the narrow strip between the fields
and the road, a squatter's camp of Rom,
two-room two-storied peaked-roof houses
of sticks and boards, gaps big enough
to make the interiors plainly visible.
No furniture, sleeping pallets upstairs,
bundles in bare rooms down,
the two floors linked by exterior ladders.
Outside snowy laundry bleached on lines,
a woman washed her naked boy
with water from a bucket, food steamed
in pots hung over fires. Everything orderly,
everything neat. Our bus stopped for us to ogle.
No gypsy returned our stares. Instead, one man
mooned our impudence, most appropriately
gave us his disdainful backside.

# The Thing about Life

It's a strange thing about life—
how we want it, no matter what—
the cane, the hearing aid,
the oxygen pulled along behind us
like a grocery cart, which, of course,
it sort of is, feeding us our necessaries.
For the fortunate, the brain continues to function
at more or less its accustomed pace—
a little clog, a blockage here and there,
but we manage to work around them,
process and produce. Through
my thicker lenses, around my
growing cataracts, I still am able to see
the hummingbird, iridescent green speck
riding purple-leaved branch of the plum tree
in early morning breeze. Behind them
once again the sun clears the mountain.

# In Purest Marble

A naked female figure on a tufted cushion
reclines gracefully on her side. We linger
to study her long perfect back, lovely buttocks,
   folded legs tangled in a downy stone coverlet,
          feet one atop the other,
              the soles smooth and unmarked.

On folded arms her sleeping face is turned towards us.
For centuries the disbelieving have touched the cushion's
edges to prove to themselves the sculpture was indeed
stone upon stone, not luminous living flesh
                  at rest on a soft bed.
Fingers have left dark smudges on the otherwise
        unsullied white.

Eager to see continued perfection, we circle the statue,
discover
      a different perfection,
          a fully formed hermaphrodite,
       exposed, so vulnerable—we wish for a silk robe
to spread softly over the figure,
          to cover her/his tender assailable nakedness.

*The Borghese Hermaphroditus, a 2nd century AD Roman copy of a Greek
original, has been in the Louvre since 1807. The buttoned mattress upon
which the statue rests was sculpted by Gian Lorenzo Bernini in 1620.*

# Particulars

It's only the first month of the year
but already a gray titmouse has come
to check out the birdhouse that hangs
above a deep pile of snow. She examines
the tin roof from above and below, tests
the little porch, enters the round door,
backs out, enters again, tufted head tilts
quizzically from one side to the other.

The birdhouse, a whimsical piece
by a retired iron worker in Michigan,
doesn't need an occupant  to be
interesting—a carved open-mouthed
alligator swerves in a breeze midway
down the hanging wire. The bird
ignores a polka-dotted hippo whose
belly has been made into an open door,
and naked human figures painted rough
on the sides of the house, fraying yellow
yarn their hair. We'll soon know if
this construction is to her liking.

My grandfather often admonished me
to love only people, not things, but
I can't help it—I love the bird,
the birdhouse, the snow, the blue sky—
all around me every day so much beauty.
It would seem to be a terrible ingratitude
not to love them.

# Gary Swaim

widely-published poet, produced playwright, published fiction writer, and digital painter, received his A.B. in English from the University of California, Riverside and his Ph.D. in Comparative Literature and Philosophy from the University of Redlands and Claremont Graduate University. Currently, a faculty member in the Master of Liberal Studies program at Southern Methodist University, he has taught broadly across the United States, and is the founding Executive Editor of *Pony Express(ions)*, an online literary journal for S.M.U. Dr. Swaim is a Minnie-Stevens Piper Professor of Excellence for the state of Texas.

# Black and White Rag

"Do not play this piece fast.
It is never right to play Ragtime fast."
—Scott Joplin

Let it play lentando
in Chicago's searing heat.
Treat it andantino
to Miami's brooding beat.
Syncopate the cadence,
counter every black with white.
Make them taste soulful rhythm
in my Ragtime dirge tonight.

I wrote it jeremiad
with white keys laid on black,
so let it play itself sad
the sole song in town, Jack.
It's one man on the treble
and one man on the bass,
as each plays his cleft to the color of his face.

Play appassionato,
it's wrong to play it fast.
Yea, slip it in the marrow,
slow. . .gentle to the last.
A black man's soul brought down hard
in the face of a white man's spite,
that's my syncopated score
to be settled by tonight.

# Paradise Lost

Eve drank the last
of the Old Bushmill.

I've used my only Viagra.
Watched like a dead tree

as my Nortel dropped forty
friggin' points in half a day.

Every bone in my arthritic body
aches like I was snake bit.

Can't make a backhand volley
to save my ass.

Acid reflux last
night from some strange fruit I ate.

What's next God? You gonna
give me a criminal son in my old age?

# Colors

Lighting on bright thistles, aster, and joe-pye weed,
a diminutive Painted Lady thrusts an even brasher color
on her world. A flash of orange against prickly reds and purples.
Morning incandescence unmatched at the sun's rising.

Though it's flamboyant orange you first see, mistaking the black
bruise-looking patches for dark leaves on which she rests,
the light of clearer day shows murky colors with bright—
fearsome beauty.

Someone has said dark stains streaking the butterfly's wings
come from the male's violent love making and serve as weights to keep
his Painted Lady from flying away.

# Orange Popsicle

My mouth is desert dry.
Blowing sand dunes coat the palate,
diminutive grains make gaudy sounds
between upper molars #2 and 3 and lower
#'s 30 and 31. I can't swallow. I wash bits
of sand about the mouth with the only saliva
I can muster.

From across the hall in our ICU,
Room 318, Mr. Leland shouts, "How 'bout
some food? Bring me *something* to eat."
From Room 322 it's the almost inaudible voice
of Mrs. Kreutzer whispering, "Just a piece of toast,
please. A piece of toast," and the wind pushes
what seems a Sisyphean boulder up the side of my

left, lower wisdom tooth wall, only to fall back into
the cavity of the adjoining tooth. Oh, if I could
only swallow, but tubes populate my throat—desert snakes
twisting joyously down my throat and back to the ventilator
giving me life.

I hear her walking the hallway, high heels clipping
a light fantastic on a clinically white floor.
"Who needs an orange popsicle? Oranges for sale,"
she sings waggishly. And, at last, I am able to swallow,
as I now must swallow many things, especially fear.

# Collecting Pieces

Still, at this late age in life, I look
for separate pieces of my soul,

scattered, I believe, like shards
of pottery across the land.

Once, I dug in an Italian farmer's field,
in sludge following hard rain, hands

reaching deep into rich, black mud,
bringing up darkened bits of tile

from ancient Roman roofs, even
an Etruscan amphora pot handle.

It's like that, I believe. Were I to find
a shard of my soul here,  one there, then

another and another, until every single piece
of who I am fit together, making the whole,

Would I, on looking at the assemblage,
be reluctant at being placed on an artful stand,

shown to the world?

# Critical Analysis

She said it was a novel
as she began reading
from her  manuscript.

But, I heard the voice
of Rilke. I hear Rilke all the time,
of course, so I thought "my problem"

and bought the idea of a novelist
warming to her audience, reading
fiction in a rich alto voice, until

I heard  the speaker of her narrative say,
"My father, when I was only four, grabbed
me by the collar, threw me against

the wall, and broke my femur."
After a slight break in her voice
and a longer hesitation before the next

sentence, I knew this was not a Rilke caesura,
knew this was not fiction,  knew it was
a memoir in a child's full body cast.

# Three-Penny Nails

*—for Pop, 10/15/1914 - 9/20/2005*

I should have a hammer in my hand
3-penny nails at the ready, or my fingernails
black with transmission grease from one of those
big rigs that hauls freight East down Interstate 8.
Maybe I need to shave a wood shim to keep the refrigerator
from rocking every time I open its door to get some milk.

I don't do those things.  Never been able to make my fingers
work like that very well.  Mine fit slick, black computer
keys or # 2 pencils — words, words, words

> that fail me now as I contemplate
> my father's death

With him gone, after nearly ninety-one years, who will build
fences, who will be certain that window jambs are square, who'll
fix the washing machines of the earth? I'm the only one who knows, but
the world's at the very edge of utter disintegration.

# A Reading

She was an apparition
as she materialized before
her audience wearing literary
dignity like a cloak wrapped blackly
about a thin frame.  She read, light
frothy poems at first, evoking mandatory
titters from a gathering of knowing listeners
dressed in polite gray.  Then she set them aside,
audience and poems alike, like single sheets
of thin, frivolous paper, and reached deep
down where vital organs live.

Miniature narratives she called
them, exercises, warm-ups for the big stuff,
stuff that stumbles into anthologies to be
read by freshmen frocked in pink
in Biloxi, Mississippi.

She read with a certain casualness
at first, adjusting occasionally, dark stringy
hair falling over her equally dark-rimmed
glasses.  Something about a woman sitting
in an empty house listening for the closing
of a door, I think.  I didn't really hear
the words.  But I tasted them.  Acrid
to the tongue, frightened, desolate.
And as they wore on, with a certain tragic
theatricality, I thought she grew noticeably
uncertain of words her own pale lips formed,
as if too bitter for the mouth, too painful
for her ears, too lonely to be so.  Momentarily,

she stopped, turned her back on an audience
long forgotten, just remembered,
and gathered what composure could
be gathered into the small white school-teacher
blouse I now noticed she was wearing.
Turning back again, eyes yet moist, showing
a soft blue embarrassment, she suggested someone
else might need to finish her little story, but
the silence pushed her on to the very last
word, when she vanished from her listeners
only to be seen two years later in a new
literary anthology, under short fiction.

# Weeping Arm[1]

Don't look to the eyes.
They're dry, cerulean blue
set deeply in my blanched and hoary
 rice paper face.  Strangely, it's my swollen arm
that's crying, crying for my country, ravaged by politicians,
both right and left, running at one another with sharp blades.
Tears are thin salve for the soul,
Shrieking and slashing go on and on.

*** 

"Yours is not an emotional malady," the physician says.
"It's only a matter of small error.  The needle (the Lumen)
 placed in your left arm missed its intended mark, thus the recurring
weeping from your arm. It cries as if eyes to the heart."

"The Loman? The *Willy* Loman? You placed *that* in my arm?"

"No, but that, too, gives rise to crying."


[1]Weeping arm is a medical condition in which an arm, usually, becomes very swollen owing to edema  resulting from an injury of one
sort or another.  Frequently, the edema seeps through the flesh, ap-
pearing  like tears.

# What Night Questions

He breathes complications of night
like a World War I trench veteran,
mustard gas blocking air passages.
He endures inquisitions at the hands
of unknown enemies, my dying father,
while he tries to calm brittle, restless legs.

———

Had you expected to live forever?

No. I thought I'd see the sun
fall just once more into the blue lake
and push concentric circles of light beneath
my feet at the shore.

Why are you frightened?

I feel the pulse in my thinned neck. It pounds
at first, then again and again. I wait for an eruption
in my brain. Then, the pulse falls quiet.
I hear no pulse.

But there is more you are not telling me.

My sons tell me I should not be afraid, that I am
a good man. In the middle of the night, I am not
sure.

———

He drags anxious thoughts through labyrinths
of night, weighted packs pulling at him
until he can carry them no more.

Wearied, he lays them down
        down — and with this done
                his tattered form rises above days, above nights,
                        mingles with sheerness of air, of light.

# Six Measured Months, 2006

## May
Ken Lay guts Enron and five-thousand lives.
Mel Gibson screams anti-Semitic virulence then
apologizes, of course. Gunter Grass admits
membership in the Nazi SS. I sleep.

## June
Episcopal Church names a woman its leader.
Iraq mission still not accomplished. Bang the drums.
Palestinians and Israelites trash the peace talks, again.
Three Guantanamo detainees cinch ropes about their necks,
 swing from low-hanging rafters. I still sleep.

## July
Saddam Hussein, fed by tube for weeks (not unlike I)
is dead. I stir and smile, I'm told. Stem cell research bill
passes, 63-37.  Bush vetoes. I feel a scowl crawl my face.
Ken Lay dies, coronary artery disease.  Sure. And, my stubbed
toe put me in ICU.  I turn onto my side.

## August
Nothing happens. . .or. . .maybe now, I just don't care.
I turn to my other side.

## September
U.S. marks five-year anniversary of terrorist attack, 9/11.
Let me sleep all this away. How "the world is too much
with us." The Illinois Governor has just been sentenced
to six months for racketeering. Welcome back to awareness.
The Pope reads a 14th century manuscript, decrying Islam
as evil and  inhuman." Rolling over, going back to sleep.

## October
Hamas and Fatah tear pieces of Palestine away, leaving
10 dead, 100 wounded.  I am awake and bathed with sadness.
A lone gunman enters an Amish school, kills three children.
I'm being prepared for dismissal. I fear the world outside
these walls.

# Andy's Apologia

## I.

Andy's attempt at words moves through spittle, imperceptible—
moist.
A towering spire over diminished mother and father, his motions
rag-doll
him from one side of the room to the other, nervously: gangly
giraffe lolling
among other aimless beasts of the world. He is forty, going on
seven,

perhaps less. No one knows for sure. It's known only that on
most days
he inhabits his gawky form with grace. No one confuses
this day, however, with just any day. Andy will be baptized.
He will reel under the weight of a significance he'll not understand.

Raw inelegance. No grace.
On the savanna, such a lonely living thing would, in confusion,
be prey to the lion. But here, Andy will be surrounded
by well-intentioned ones who'll claw at his innocent, empty head,

use sharpened theologies to pull his carcass into water, and drown
him
with love.

## II.

He is down, deep down in water where blue cotton candy floats
beneath eyelids and cold waves blouse loose white cloth
about arms and legs and chest. Filaments of hair rise...fall...twist
in frightened lives of their own.

And Andy is unknowing, a timorous animal held under water
by officious, ecclesiastical hands though he can only guess why.
His body pleads for release, reaches for air, but is pulled lower and
lower
until he knows the release must be his: *Give in, give way! Let it gush*
up through nostrils—down through throat, wash away my loneliness,
take me where I can understand something. . .anything at all.

**III.**

His form rises to the surface, pure white flotsam.
He steps from the pool, feels the cloth clasp about his body,
constricting blood flow to every part of him.
The minister intones resonant words of consolation:

"You are saved, saved. Dear Andy, you are saved,"
and Andy looks longingly back, into deep. . .deep candy-blue
water.

## Rider of Asses

I read but a line from a Rilke poem
("I want to become like one of those
who through the night go driving
wild horses.") and I am struck dumb.
St. Paul thrown from an ass, voice
scaled like eyes at the sound of racing
hoofbeats.

I go without sound to the village
of Damascus where I fast and pray
and wonder that words can ever come
again. I move my lips. I run fingers
through the dirt at my feet, shaping syllables
(Hebrew, Greek, and Aramaic) but not even the simple
beauty of one Rilke word. I'm a rider of asses
and can't voice the dazzle of wild horses.

# The Lesson

Breath smelling of Sen-Sen, sweet—licorice,
weight of a sable, 120-bass Excelsior accordion hanging
about his shoulders, black albatross.  He leans to the boy

playing ragged, wheezing D-scales with small, clumsy fingers.
His own, long like unspooled thread, glide over imagined Steinway keys—
Carnegie, Albert Hall.  Rachmaninoff's *Piano Concerto No. 3*.

Napoleon Brandy dreams.  All his life he dreams.
Shocks of silk and velvet at his wrists, brightly ringed fingers.
A quickness of light.  Audiences of other places and times.

# Cleaning Slates

—for Jim Paul


It flowered mercilessly inside him
                              that deadly dahlia
planting roots in first one organ

then another, blooming for all
to see when it broke flesh
meant to conceal fearsome truths.

"I would tell you about my pain, if I could talk.
My throat won't let me speak.
I cannot speak.


"I would sing a verse of *Ring of Fire*
maybe two or three of *Peggy Sue*,
strum badly the few guitar chords I know

and sing a histrionic bass to
*A Church in the Valley by the Wildwood*,
but I can't sing, so tell me why I'm here.

"Let me go.  Let East Texas rains
wash the slate clean on which I now write.
Let me go to where words will resonate

with any cloud that will listen, where bass
will match and direct the thunderous choir
of summer storms

"Don't be concerned for me.  I'll be busy
making some more deals for rain.
Everyone needs some slate washing in his life.

Each day fresh, each day full.
I'll be busy.  Might even learn to get an $A^7$
out of this old battered guitar."

# Acknowledgements

Poetry is a very private preoccupation. At another level, it is the most collaborative of efforts, shared among writer, reader and publisher. We wish to express sincere appreciation to these Presses for allowing selected poems to be published in this collection.

## Alan Birkelbach

*descant*
San Pedro River Review
Blue Rock Review
Texas Poetry Calendar 2013

## Nathan Brown:

Village Books Press
Mezcalita Press

## Tony Mares:

Wings Press
Placitas, New Mexico: Voices from the American Land, Vol. II

## Ron Moore:

Current
*descant*

## Karla K Morton:

Finishing Line Press
Texas Review Press
Blue Horse Press

## Elizabeth Raby:

San Angelo State University, Virtual Artists Collective
Alzheimer's Poetry Project

## Gary Swaim:

Ardent!
The Mayo Review